Family Circle of Cats

Linda L. R. Bennett

LifeRich Publishing is a registered trademark of
The Reader's Digest Association, Inc.

LifeRich Publishing books may be ordered
through booksellers or by contacting:

LifeRich Publishing
1663 Liberty Drive
Bloomington, IN 47403
www.liferichpublishing.com
844-686-9607

ISBN: 978-1-4897-4107-3 (sc)
ISBN: 978-1-4897-4108-0 (e)

Print information available on the last page.

LifeRich Publishing rev. date: 03/23/2022

Contents

Introduction

We were a family of humans but, in addition, cats were an important part of our lives. Our feline family became an integral part of the family unit when John and I married. Initially we did not search for these companions but, early on, each inadvertently entered our lives providing more than we could have ever expected at the onset of their appearance. The dimension of their importance is rather hard to explain. Yet the full measure of the devotion of the individual pets left an indelible mark in our hearts.

Before our marriage John, my husband, had a special love for cats. From accounts relayed by the Bennett family, his affection was apparent even when he was a child. He bandaged an injured cat meticulously wrapping cloth on the source of the cat's wound but all his efforts were soon undone and the cat scurried away. Cats were a presence at mealtime and scraps of food were generously given to an eagerly awaiting cat under the dining table. He was often observed with cats "finding" him rather than his seeking them. I don't recall specific names of these friends but I suspect each had its own distinguishing identity.

As far as I was concerned, cats were a part of my life while growing up. The first I remember about the little creatures happened when I was about three years old and I found a litter of kittens in a storage building; unfortunately, I fell from their sanctuary ultimately ending with a nasty cut close to my left eye. A few years later, after settling in a new residence, Buttercup, a yellow kitten, was given to the family but she didn't stay with us probably finding another home. Another unknown kitty was donated from my grandparents' farm but disappeared en route to our house. Wiggles, who made a forever space in my heart, next entered my life and, regrettably, fell prey to neighborhood dogs. To culminate my association with cats, Rascal was a kitten whose mother decided to have her litter at my family's house and he stayed until we moved away.

During the first year of our marriage, we, for a brief time, had gold fish which succumbed to my overfeeding them. Then, after our little girls were toddlers, an associate of John's relatives told us that a dachshund/ Pekinese puppy needed a home and encouraged John and me to take him. The little dog was adorable.

Therefore he came into our lives for a few years only to leave without our really ever understanding what happened to him.

Thus the background for forthcoming decades we shared in the incredible journey of our extended family – the family circle of cats. Their stories mirror the chronicles paralleling the lives we were living during the time with our feline family.

Shadow

Two little girls were distraught after their precious dog disappeared. Dawn started kindergarten about the same time we realized he was forever gone, but, after numerous attempts to find him, we realized we would not see him again. Tracy was especially at loose ends because she did not have her sister/playmate at home every day during the week. However the neighbor, who lived in the house behind ours, had a wonderful sweet natured mother cat, White Paws. A the beginning of that school year White Paws had a litter of kittens which became for Tracy a nice diversion and source of a resolution to the girls' lost pet.

Watching and playing with four little kittens became entertainment for Tracy when she was outofdoors while her sister/playmate was at school. Soon, in the afternoons, Dawn was enthralled by the sweet active furry creatures. All of the kittens seemed to have their mother's amiable disposition making each one a true joy and immediately, after the encouragement from the neighbor lady, a natural decision was made – a kitten became a permanent part of our family.

Two of the kittens were black and the other two were gray tabby with white the same as their mother's coloring. I don't recall why the girls decided on a black one but the choice was made (the neighbor lady said we could take another one but we thought we would be better with only one). Everyone was delighted, including the girls' parents. Days of sadness from the missing pet were replaced with new invigoration as we watched the kitten take his place in our family and his new home. Because of his black coat and his following us everywhere the little fellow was named Shadow (Dawn had also ben enamored by the correlation of shadows and reflection in pools of water when we took nature walks; she said reflections were like shadows but in color; and the many times the poem "My Shadow" was read to our daughters provided to the chosen name).

Shadow adjusted to his surroundings without any problems; he seemed to be a good fit for all. He was energetic and curious indicative of his innate nature. However, during his first Christmas season when John and I returned from a staff Christmas party we could not find Shadow under the house garage where we placed him before we left. After looking in every nook and cranny, we noticed a small opening under the closed garage door. As this point I frantically searched outside the house calling as I walked. Finally, I heard a faint mew and I saw this small black mass perched on a top branch of a tall tree in our yard. I continued to coax him to come down but Shadow was terrified and snow was beginning to fall rapidly. The neighbor lady came to the rescue by asking her teenage son for help. The boy took a ladder and climbed up to retrieve our shaking and cold little baby. All was well. We were grateful to the teen for his assistance but I really don't who was happier, the little girls, the parents or the kitten when he returned to his safe and warm home.

Within a few years we moved to Cape Girardeau, Missouri. At this point Shadow had become a young adult cat. As he grew our affection grew with him. His personality continued to exhibit that of his mother: he was loving, sociable and smart. In mornings he learned to nuzzle with his nose on their chins to awaken his girls before they left their beds. He "knocked "at the front porch door telling us he wanted inside. He was a lap cat, purring as contented he could be. Through it all, the move, etc., he adapted to his family and we to him.

After a while Shadow moved with us from Cape Girardeau but the move incurred some difficult changes for him. He had been an indoor/outdoor cat surrounded by freedom. At our new home Shadow was confined to the indoors. Also, his girls were busy with school and the parents were, much of the day, away at work leaving Shadow, for most part, alone. A permanent decision was made - Shadow needed a new home.

The grandparents thought Shadow was a very special cat and they agreed to take him to live with them. Giving him up was heart rendering for our family but we knew he would be safe with love from another caring family. Therefore, for the rest of his life, he was given adoring attention which included the best food, freedom, security and companionship (including evening walks as he followed the grandparents down the lane in front of their house). Nonetheless he always was happy when we came for visits finding welcoming laps from his previous people to enjoy his company; he seemed to remember us and, in some real ways, we remained forever a part of his life.

Missy

After locating to a different town, our family realized we had a void in the family. Something was missing and we knew what. Within a short time John learned a good family were willing to give away a half-grown cat named Missy. Dawn and Tracy were ectastic. Immediately, upon seeing her, we decided she should be ours. She was a beautiful fluffy long haired tourtoise shell (a blending of yellow/orange, black and gray) with golden eyes. She had a loving and sweet disposition. She was just what we wanted. Our family was complete again even though we saw Shadow frequently.

The girls were so excited that they did not want to be separated from Missy. We even took her in the car when we made a quick trip to a grocery store close to our house. The girls stayed in the car while a purchase was made but, when the car door opened, Missy ran from us. We called and called for her and searched to no avail. Time passed. We thought the cat was gone. At this point both daughters were crying with both parents almost in tears. We returned home sad and disappointed.

The next morning two young girls were reluctantly taken to school. All the hope for a loving companion seemed to vanish. Nonetheless I decided to look once again for the wandering feline. After purchasing, at the store, a can of fishy smelly cat food I opened the can and proceeded to entreat her in the wooded area behind the store. My hand was extended as far as possible among the trees. I was beginning to lose heart when I saw some leaves rustling and heard a meow – out came the cat. I picked her up holding her close to me tightly. What a joyous reunion that afternoon following school! The new family member was back home.

A few months passed. Missy seemed to settle in her new home. However she left for some weeks and, again, we found ourselves cat-less. We tried to locate her but we couldn't find her. We missed her so much that we decided to get a kitten. From the local newspaper we saw an ad which read, "Free kittens to a good home." We wasted no time in getting the kitten, a tiny white ball of fur. We excitedly took him home. The next morning Missy was waiting at our house door wanting to come in – we had gone from no cats to two!

Another surprise came. A few weeks later Missy presented her family with four frisky kittens, two long haired yellow ones and two tortoise shell the same as Missy. As soon as possible homes were found for the babies. The decision was made to have Missy spayed. Again, we were back to permanently having two cats (there is more to the story about the white kitten).

Later Missy's life became somewhat more traumatic. When she was probably four years old, I started to drive Dawn and Tracy to visit friends when I turned the key in the car's ignition some strange sounds emitted from under the car's hood. I looked to see about the problem. Missy had evidently crawled inside resulting with a leg caught under a fan belt. Perplexed I called my teenaged cousin who came with an assortment of tools and diligently tried to help. Fortunately my husband happened to come home. He pulled up the fan belt which immediately released the cat's leg. A terrified Missy promptly fled and we did not find her until our neighbor was alerted to the barking dog at their storage building. Missy had taken refuge from her devastating mishap. Again, a can of smelly cat food came to rescue as Dawn persuaded our kitty to come out from under the building. Missy had to have short portion amputated from the injured leg but she returned to a full life that included climbing trees.

Our family life continued with Missy and her "brother" and the changes we incurred. She was an affectionate and endearing family member. Missy lived for 15 or 16 years in which time she was a constant companion through moves to Tennessee, Missouri and, finally, Arkansas. She provided so many memories: the Christmas tree ornaments that she removed from the tree and played with during the night while her family slept; waking me each morning with one of her soft velvet-like paws touching gently on my cheek and then proceeding to the kitchen to be fed (no one else was awakened but she made sure to wake me); an upset and crying friend of mine who came to our home when Missy jumped on her lap as she meowed and rubbed on the friend in sympathy (Missy sensed her despair); the sweet naps she took cuddled next to her adopted brother; she and her brother seemed always to know the arrival time for their girls coming from school and waited on a stool which John placed in front the living room window announcing their arrival (even after the girls went to college the two cats would meow as the girls could be seen approaching home); and so many more incidences of her precious life with us. Missy continued in the tradition of Shadow by being forever an entrenched part of our family with lasting memories.

Mister

(Mister Cat)

After Missy came Mister (we decided if we had a Missy our new male should be called Mister) or rather the lives of the two intermingled because most of their lives meshed with each other. Mister was a tiny white rat-looking ball of fur when we selected him. He was an "accident" resulting from a pedigree Siamese mother wandering away for a short time from her home. With his special lineage he inherited the typical loud distinctive meow of his mother. From the beginning, at our home, he was spirited and extremely curious more than we had observed in other cats. He immediately adopted Missy as a possible surrogate parent even though at that time Missy had kittens of her own. Nonetheless each of the two cats assumed its place in our family. Mister was good for us.

As Mister grew, his personality manifested itself.

He loved being with the family but adventure became a characteristic which in turn was a life style for him. Even before he developed into a young adult cat, he left our home for a few days and subsequently returned with a broken back leg; fortunately he found his way home soon enough for us to take him to the vet and surgery for a pin was put in the injured leg. Within a few months, during those early years, another episode startled me when this white cat appeared dragging a black snake in his mouth - the great white hunter cat! Birds had a way of entering the house which Mister deposited under the bed. Chipmunks were found on numerous occasions by the house doors, mostly still alive. He proved to be a source of unanticipated excitement for his human family.

Mister was fearless. Dogs were not a detriment to his world. In fact. a jogging neighbor, with his dog running with him, learned about our white cat's bravery. Our house was located on a circle drive, a perfect path for a daily jog. The neighbor regularly ran around the perimeters of the drive but on one occasion the man and dog, a dog about the size of Mister, were accosted by our cat. Immediately, after the attack, the little dog jumped into the owner's arms at which the jogger said, "He doesn't like dogs – right?" I think the man refrained from taking the route again.

Over the years Mister and Missy were mostly the cats of Dawn and Tracy. John and I certainly gave them our share of attention but when the daughters were home the cats could be found with them. The cats seemed to know the time the school bus arrived in front of our house and they waited, either by the front window or door, to greet their homecoming. The two felines were never disappointed. They were whisked away to wherever to get the proper attention they deserved.

John was doing extensive out-of-town travel for the time we lived in St Louis. Once the daughters were in college, Mister became closer to John and seemed to monitor his trips away from home. Invariably, when he saw an opened piece of luggage, Mister would position himself right on top of the packed articles and stayed until he was picked up only to jump right back. When John returned from a trip he was welcomed by Mister's Siamese yowl and proceeded to follow him from one room to another until John picked him up to be petted.

Mister assumed his dominate place in our household. He had no hesitation in getting whatever he wanted. He was known to sample any food which was left out. He was not picky. More than once he even savored donuts that were wrapped for his humans. However he certainly had no aversion to the cat food bought for him. He learned to be an assertive cat and was mostly concerned with his desires.

Mister made our lives full of amazing episodes (including his walking across the roof of our home and resisting our pleading for him to come down). He was spirited but he was sweet and loving. His affection for each of us was always evident; he savored to be on a lap purring in his loud purr showing his satisfaction. His legacy was everlasting in our hearts. We loved all aspects of his persona even the times when he gave us fright from his shenanigans

Fortunately Mister was a part of our lives for almost nineteen years (if had survived a few more weeks). Dawn and Tracy were children during the time Mister was at our home. He watched them as they left to attend college. He moved with us from Missouri to Tennessee and back, and again to Tennessee and on to Arkansas. We were so blessed for his long life and he will always occupy a distinct place in our hearts.

Cassie

(Mary Cassett)

John and I experienced a profound loss after both Missy and Mister were gone. We had not been catless for many years. With both daughters away in graduate studies the emptiness in our hearts seemed even greater. However Dawn came to visit in an autumn and, after doing some inquiring, we learned a local woman was searching for homes for kittens, that were about ten weeks old, and she was bringing them to a local vet for viewing. We did not hesitate. The three of us went to see about another kitten for our family.

The kittens were adorable. After seeing the litter we chose one beautiful little female. She was long – haired, cream-colored with dark brown appointments on her ears, paws, face and a fluffy tail which she carried regally over her back. But her most beguiling features were incredibly light blue eyes. We knew she was the

one for us. We were thrilled to take her into our home –
she couldn't take the places of our other cats but we
thought we had a spot just for her.

Such a unique and gorgeous creature deserved a
name befitting her. With my interest in art and the cat
being female, we decided to name her after an American
artist. Thus she became Mary Cassett or, rather, Cassie.
One might say she had a little bit of temperament similar
to a stereotypical artist. She had definite attitudes about
the way she wanted things to be. Her home was her
abode and immediately she established herself in it.
She did enjoy being on a lap. All food seemed to meet
her approval. The new family was accepted with no
reservations. But her personality did not accept just
everyone else who came - she ran for the closest bed to
hide under when the doorbell rang or someone entered
the house. Nonetheless we loved our little beautiful pet
and welcomed her with opened arms. In some ways she
was like a princess; she seemed to think she had a touch
of royalty about her.

Of course John knew instinctively ways to ingratiate
himself to Cassie. She followed him around the house
whenever he was home. Sometimes he took her outside
to let her explore the yard but, when he called for her
to come, she didn't hesitate to run to him. She could
look at John with those incredible blue eyes and knew

he would respond to her beckon call. There was truly a mutual admiration between the two of them.

Thanksgiving arrived after we acquired Cassie. Cassie did not understand all the goings-on surrounding the holiday. We invited family and some extended family as well. During all the busyness of preparation for the usual feast we lost track of Cassie's whereabouts. No one realized we had not seen her for quite a while before or after the big meal until later we looked for her and couldn't find her anywhere she normally could have been. All of us were involved with cleanup from the dinner when I happened to open a lower cupboard door. Out emerged our frightened wide-eyed ball of fur! She had found a hiding place for seclusion from all the hubbub, people and activity of the day. Cassie was being Cassie (many times Cassie learned to entertain herself with undoing toilet paper from the rolls and running down the hall with the paper trailing behind).

After a few months we adopted another kitten. From the onset of the new arrival, Cassie asserted herself to be dominate; she was still the little princess in the household. As they grew to be adult cats Cassie remained the smaller of the two but size was no deterrent to her getting the bluff on the new family member. She waited for him at the wall corner as he approached her from down the hallway and subsequently proceeded to attack him with stiletto-like paws. The victimized cat immediately ran to get away from the pint-sized foe. He was friendly. She was not, to put it mildly (another evidence of the rivalry from Cassie occurred after she saw the other cat playing on the floor with a candy cane which had fallen off the Christmas; she proceeded to knock a candy cane from the tree).

Cassie and her adopted brother were special in our hearts. The evenings John and I enjoyed time with the two on our laps as we relaxed, Cassie on John's lap and the other cat on mine. Listening to soft purring sounds which emanated from these adorable creatures along with stroking and petting their heads gave so much pleasure to us (also Cassie could be found watching birds, other animals and tennis matches, occasionally batting her paws on the T.V. as the images moved across the screen). Even though the cats were not especially friends, we had become their family and they were satisfied being with us.

One of the summer sessions in graduate school, I lived away from home on campus at the university. While I was gone Cassie developed a problem that required surgery at the animal hospital. Her sprit was indomitable but evidently her little body was delicate and she died. She was no more than five years old. After the long lives of the preceding cats we were so sorry to have to say goodbye so soon to the little princess cat.

Newcombe

(John Newcombe)

John Newcombe was Cassie's house mate. John, my husband, saw an ad in the local newspaper stating an owner had grey tabby kittens for a good home. He evidently, being the cat lover he was, thought a little tiger kitten would be a nice addition. Thus Newcome joined Cassie in our family.

Upon seeing the kitten John was charmed. The little one was not all that small. In fact, even though he was still very young, he was quite big for his age. Nonetheless the fellow had a sweet friendly personality. While we watched, the kitten scampered with his brothers. He epitomized a picture of health (he had been well cared for). I immediately knew we would take the new addition to our home. John had the perfect name for him: John Newcombe, the name of a great tennis player. At this point Cassie didn't realize her life was changing.

John was enthralled. He wanted Tracy, who at that time lived in the same town, to meet this wonderful animal. We took him over to her home before we actually introduced him to Cassie and his new surroundings. He was met with approval. John and I were both pleased to have two cats once again fill our hearts with feline affection. Cassie was not quite as excited.

From the beginning Newcombe was an amiable and good natured kitty. He seemed to adapt to his environment immediately with no qualms. I don't recall any separation issues when we took him but, on arrival to our house, we learned Cassie was in control of the Bennett residence. She very soon asserted herself letting all of us know Newcombe was only tolerated by her and she was the number one cat. Newcombe seemed to acquiesce. Nothing changed his demeanor. He was perfectly satisfied with all of us.

Newcombe and Cassie lived harmoniously (on more than one occasion we even found the two of them napping in the same chair), under Cassie's watchful eye, for the next years. John and I loved our very different personality cats and we assumed they would have the long lives that Missy and Mister had had but, unfortunately, Cassie's life was cut short. Newcombe became an only cat which didn't seem to bother him.

Nonetheless, again, there was a lacking in our

lives. The vet assistant, at the animal clinic, realized we wanted another pet to live with Newcombe and her mother cat had kittens including a calico. John was away attending a meeting when the call came about the little one. When he telephoned me, we decided to bring another cat into our family. Newcombe had a new little sister.

After a brief period of adjustment, our home was once again filled with two cats; we never lost the love for Cassie but we loved the new addition in a special way. Newcombe continued to be Newcombe. Nothing ever seemed to upset him, for the most part. Life was good for him. He just lived the way he wanted to live and accepted his world as if he was grateful for whatever he had. In fact, my Mother, who had a soft spot in her heart for him, commented that he was the best natured cat she had ever seen. Her assessment about Newcombe apparently was true. Nonetheless, even though the cats didn't conflict much with each other, they never developed the closeness of Missy and Mister.

One Thanksgiving John and I didn't have family coming. Never fear we had family with the cats. Newcombe's adopted sibling and he partook of a typical feast with all the trimmings: turkey, cornbread dressing, giblet graving and more. Their meal was even given to them on a platter which was placed on a placemat (no napkins, however). After eating to their hearts' content, they found the most comfortable place in their home and took a typical after Thanksgiving nap. It was a good day (and they, along with John and me) enjoyed leftovers for quite a while afterward.

Only once did Newcombe show he was frustrated. He always stayed close to his home even though he did like to be outdoors; he mostly roamed in the backyard or stretched out on the driveway. However, one day I allowed our confident cat to come indoors as he yowled in an untypical pitched meow. When he entered the garage I knew the reason for his dilemma: a skunk had moved in front of Newcombe spaying him as went by. The odor was not only offensive to me but poor Newcombe was appalled by the smell and didn't know what to do. Fortunately we proceeded to the animal hospital, even though I hated for the vet to clean and deodorize him (also he was due for his yearly inoculations), but, thankfully, he was all right with no trace of the skunk encounter.

We developed a loving relationship with Newcombe as we did the other family cats. We believed he would be with us for a longer time than actually happened. He acquired a virus that was incurable. He was twelve years old and we had to give him up leaving a vacant spot as happened with our other family cats. We loved him so much.

Libry

Libry was an adopted sibling for Newcome, after Cassie's passing. She was a little orphan calico kitten (her mother had been accidently killed) and fulfilled the empty area for us once we were without Cassie. The vet assistant at the animal clinic realized we were saddened by the loss of Cassie. She had a litter of kittens that needed homes and she called telling us about little Libry. John was out of town. When he phoned I told him about the kitten. I told him if I saw her she would be ours. True to my nature I brought her home with me. Libry was the name chosen; it was a shortened version of the word library, my occupation as a librarian.

Libry was so tiny that we kept her in the bath tub for a number of weeks after we brought her home because we were afraid we would inadvertently hurt her. Also we weren't sure how Newcombe would accept her. He was curious about something unfamiliar in the bathroom;

he often went to the closed bathroom door, batting his paw under the door trying to find what was there but he never was aggressive about her. As she grew, her residence became her domain with all its benefits afforded her.

John made the decision to have Libry declawed. I believe he thought she would do better strictly as an indoor kitty. After all she was so small and he perceived fragile when she came to live with us, she needed special consideration. As a result Libry was the only pet we ever had that never went outside and she appeared always satisfied in her life.

Libry and Newcombe did not develop a close relationship. They were not hostile toward each other but rather just maintained their own independence. In fact, in some ways, each was like being in a one cat home. Occasionally we found them together on a bed or we noticed the two in the recliner together but not cuddled up; probably Newcombe, as the older cat, learned to keep his distance from living with Cassie who kept him in line. Nonetheless Libry loved lap time as much as Newcombe. Also she welcomed anyone who came into our house.

When Newcombe died our household became a one-cat residence. Libry embraced her new role with no hesitation. She adapted quickly by following us from room- to-room whenever we were at home. She was very endearing. We learned to love this great kitty with a unique kind of tenderness.

At some point John and I noticed Libry was having problems with one of her back legs. I don't recall how she injured her leg but the vet determined to amputate the hurt appendage. Thereafter Libry functioned with only three and one half legs (reminiscent of Missy's life). No changes occurred after the procedure in her response to her surrounding; she remained the same. She was a real trooper living as though nothing had happened.

Everyday brought pleasure to us with Libry. Our lives were integrated and consumed with her for several years as she became our only cat. John especially loved carrying her in his arms and talking to her as loud purrs could be heard from her throat. Of course, she strictly stayed indoors because she was declawed but there was no indication she ever wanted to venture outside. Our home provided her contentment and all her needs were met. Again we were blessed in having another "favorite" cat and believed she would be with us many years.

In the evening after a busy day, John and I found relaxation sitting either reading or watching T.V.

Libry usually was cozily curled on John's lap. Thus

was a usual scenario for the cat and us. Life was good. However one night Libry started yowling. The evening seemed typical for us but we soon realized Libry was in pain. The next morning we took her to the animal clinic. The vet suggested she stay over the weekend and we left her.

Libry never returned home. She had shown no indications of discomfort but, unfortunately, she had acquired cancer and there was no treatment to help her. We were shocked to learn our sweet kitty had probably been ill for some time; she never complained.

Giving up another part of our cat family created a longing once again for both John and me. We missed the warmth of her both physically and emotionally. The loss was great. Another chapter to our cat family history was forth coming.

Odus and
Odenroder

Two little kittens found our home. They were
brothers from the same litter who initially lived
alone across the street at a neighbor's residence.
They were fed occasionally but they lived outside on
the front porch, for the most part, without attention or
affection. The little fellows, probably about six weeks
old or so, were friendly and lived contently, just the two
of them, under no human care. I observed them from
afar thinking they needed more food than what was
given to them. Thus begins their story.

At first, I sneaked cat food whenever the kitties had
disappeared from my view. I did not want them to see
me. However my tactics did not eventually work. I have
no idea how they learned the food was mysteriously
appearing but in a short time two tiny faces came to
the front door of our house looking over the storm door

panel – they wanted to come inside. Then I found the two snuggled together on our front porch glider. Soon our place became a permanent abode but we really had no inkling that they were adopting us until an unfortunate event happened.

These precious babies started staying with us. Even though they seemed to want into our house we just talked and petted them (and left cat food) whenever they came to the door. However an incident changed our interaction with the two. We happened to find one who had hurt a back leg. Something had to be done. Therefore we scooped up both small cats and took them to the animal clinic. There the vet had to remove a portion of the leg (reminiscent of Missy and Libry). While at the clinic we decided the kittens were our responsibility. Before we left, shots were injected, etc. and we adopted them as ours – they were even named, Odus and Odenroder (John sometimes laughingly referred to himself as those aliases).

Odus, the injured kitty, had lovely white fur interspersed with grey tabby stripes. Odenroder, the other one, was tuxedo- colored, solid black appointed with white on his face and chest. Both were truly wonderful. We loved them from those beginning moments. We had no reservations taking them even with the leg issue. Those little kittens chose us to be a permanent part of our family and we, in turn after realizing their decision, took them into our home – even though, I have not mentioned, another cat already had been living with us for about three years prior to their coming on board.

For close to three years John and I enjoyed having a multi cat home. The three fellows adapted quite well even though there was some discord between two of them toward Odus. All were accustomed to being indoors and outdoors. When I thought they should be in at night I would call their names and all three would come running. Also they would jump on the seat of the walker, a necessity after I had a broken leg, and allow me to push them from inside the house – all three at the same time. They stayed close to home lounging in the lawn or porch glider. Sometimes Odenroder could be seen in the empty concrete bird bath. But nothing was as enchanting as seeing Odenroder and Odus watching birds or falling snow at the French doors in the family room while John napped in the recliner with the other cat asleep on his lap. Yes, the times were memorable even though we had not planned on a cat family the size we acquired (I always liked a serendipity life and, again, this happened with this trio of cats). Our hearts were filled with the affection of and an abundant supply of attention which comes from all that is derived from endearing feline pets.

John was experiencing troubling health matters. Nonetheless he found an abundance of attention from the three cats. John carried, at different times, a cat around the house as he commented about loving each one; they, in turn, lavished their love on him. During those days, at least one cat was on his lap while the third napped on me when I sat on the sofa by his chair. Just at the right moments the presence of our cat family brightened his life and gave him the measure of companionship he needed as his well-being diminished.

Unfortunately, in the autumn, Odenroder was accidently struck by an automobile in the street in front of our home leaving a lacking in our hearts. Again I faced intense loss after he was gone. Odus assumed his position being a solitary little fellow; he seemed to enjoy having the whole bed by himself in finding comfort next to the pillows and the special attention he received. However, during a heavy rain storm and stormy winds before Christmas day, he disappeared after John allowed him to go outside. We never saw him again. Our lives were not the same; they were wonderful creatures in the part they played of life giving us what we needed at a particular time. But one cat was left.

L.Y.K.

The remaining cat, after the loss of Odenroder and Odus, had been acquired before the little brothers adopted us. He was already named when he came to us. His name was L.Y.K. or Little Yellow Kitten. He had been found disserted in a parking lot. Initially the orphan was taken to become a pet by the woman who found him. However the family dogs were too aggressive toward him. She and her family knew another permanent place was needed. Since we had lost Libry only a short time before, when learning of L.Y.K. and his story, again, John and I were ready to take another kitten. Our cat family had increased once again.

When L.Y.K. arrived, as we had before with the other cat family members, we were delighted. Willingly John and I accepted him. He was a healthy, lively kitten. However he had one problem - a broken tail. The previous family had taken him for the necessary shots but the tail had not been corrected. We learned the removal of a portion of the tail was essential for his well-being; he had no feeling in it and probably he would be in danger if his tail became ensnared some way. The tail was altered and L.Y.K. became a tail-less cat, a distinction which set him apart from all of the other cats.

Nonetheless L.Y.K. was not hampered by his physical mishap. This yellow/orange striped furry ball of energy quickly made himself at home. We realized in a short while, it was best not to leave him unattended. He could speed through the house in record time. Chests, tables and other furniture were no detriment, and actually a challenge, for him as he explored "his" house. The tempo definitely picked up with this pet but that meant, when were away at work, etc., he had to be confined to a room where he could do the least damage such as climbing or investigating the surroundings.

L.Y.K. was weeks old at the beginning of our life with him. He was a rather small with a friendly personality. He liked his people – all of them John, me, our daughters, sons-in-law, grandchildren and visitors to our home. He welcomed everyone to his home. However, after a short time, we realized the word "little" was inappropriate in his name because he was growing larger and larger. Thus the "Little Yellow Kitten" became the "Large Yellow Kitty" to match the size he became. No matter L.Y.K was still LY.K., including all of his entertaining antics and over-the-top personality whatever his moniker.

L.Y.K. loved John more than anyone but it could be said there was mutual attraction between the two of them. John and he played chasing tennis shoe strings which was a great sport for both of them. Then L.Y.K. started retrieving the strings taking them to John for more playing (the grandchildren enjoyed this activity at their visits). When the romps were over John was seen either carrying the cat or napping with him in the recliner; he wanted to be a part of whatever John was doing including helping prepare a Sunday school lesson. I believe, in some respects, John and L.Y.K. shared many personality characteristics that were not evident with our other cats: they both were high energy, fearless, affectionate, smart, people-oriented, confident, determined, curious, resolute, etc. Basically L.Y.K. was just the cat suited for our family when he entered our home. As time passed we realized how good his presence was for us, especially for John.

L.Y.K. showed no reticence about the two little brother kittens adopting our home. In a short time, all three cat each assumed his role in our household as if they were all meant to be here. After Odus's accident, there was a bit of animosity toward him by the other two. But there was really no major conflict among them; we certainly encouraged all of them to live harmoniously by loving them individually as well as collectively as a group. They were in our home for close to three years. We truly thought we would have them for years but, unfortunately, we lost the two brothers when they were young adult cats, much to our disappointment.

L.Y.K. continued on as the companion for John and me with John as the number one person for him. During this time John's health condition was rapidly failing. Fortunately L.Y.K. never wavered in his love for John and was his constant friend. The last months before death John became less approachable with a lack of interest in life but the cat was always the same toward John. About the same time the two of us developed a closer relationship. However I knew I could not replace what John and L.Y.K. had between them. L.Y.K. lived with John about six years previous to his demise (during the six years John and I worked on a children's book about L.Y.K. which was later published).

I am so thankful for L.Y.K.'s presence in my life after John's passing. There was a sense of continuity to existence with the cat. He started sleeping at the foot of my bed which he had not done in the past, not in my face but near my feet. He followed me throughout the house as he had when John was with us. I learned he liked yogurt as much as I and, whenever I opened a container, L.Y.K. would look at me with his eyes wanting to share. After a while he evolved into an indoor cat because he apparently hurt a back paw and I knew he needed to stay safely close to me (trips to the vet would have been an almost impossibility). For the first time in over fifty years one cat occupied our home solely with me – I was not alone.

For over four and one half years L.Y.K. and I were family. He and I grew older together. He seemed to sense the changes for both of us. Nonetheless he never stopped retrieving shoe strings from the coal bucket, which John had painted to be used as a magazine container and was later used for cat toys, to drop at his food dish. He escaped to go outside when there was an opportunity only to come to me in a short time after a brief romp. My lap provided comfort and affection for both the cat and me. The moments were filled with pleasure; John was first choice to L.Y.K. but I also knew the cat became the link to times past as well as satisfaction at the present time. He and I settled into a life style of mutual contentment. However the bliss came to a conclusion – much to my dismay.

L.Y.K. was a robust healthy kitty from the first when he was introduced to our home. But, as he approached his eleventh birthday, there were some indications he was experiencing some discomfort. At the onset, nothing seemed to bother him. However he started being somewhat reclusive; he did not sleep in my bed at night but preferred to stay in the garage. His appetite was less; he had always relished his cat food (he never declined the cat treat Temptations even while he was ill). Apparently respiratory problems manifested in him but there were no other noticeable issues. Watching this wonderful furry friend as he faltered was heartbreaking – I thought that we would be family for a long time.

The next few months brought to me the realization of losing L.Y.K. No cat had been a part of my life without John or the rest of the family and I was distraught. He was the stabilizing source of my daily life; I cared for him immensely. During the duration of his illness special food was administered to him, sometimes forcing it into his mouth. Wherever he wanted to stay, he stayed whether in his cat bed or on scatter rugs in any room of the house. I talked to him. I petted his head but I couldn't carry him because he was too large. Through it all L.Y.K. responded to whatever I tried – the cat and I grew to love each other especially when there were only the two of us. And I prayed for his being with me each day for the duration of his sickness.

The cat and I were together until his last moments. He meowed and closed his eyes as I stroked his head while I talked to him before he was taken to the vet. He seemed at peace. I am grateful for the memory.

L.Y.K. is gone. The cat family circle is complete.

The Cat
Family Circle
Redux, Etc.

The coal bucket remains on the fireplace hearth. Included in it are the cat toys collected over a fiftyyear span: assorted Christmas toys, catnip mice, chasing rods, crocheted items, balls, tennis balls, other items and, of course, tennis shoes strings which remain on the top of everything. All represent the stages of life that were shared with our individual cat family members. Laughter along with hard events is intertwined in the echoes of the past. Gratitude permeates my thoughts as I remember the joy from all of the cats we encountered on our journey.

Our human family changed. The daughters were very young as life developed into their adulthood. The family increased in number with the addition of sons-in-law and grandchildren. There was loss in many extended family loved ones. But John's death created the most notable void because of his zest for life, his adoration for family and the cat members as well. Life moves on. We are enriched in the process.

I believe our God is so immense that, not only does He love all of us, but He loves all creation more than we can fully comprehend. In the book of Genesis, from the Bible, at the beginning, all creatures were made by Him in the world, concluding with making man and then woman. Everything was perfect. He had a plan for each aspect of His creation which involved animals being under the dominion of humans. I believe His intent has not changed. We have a responsibility to care for those He created when we are given the chance. In turn cats, which become part of a family, are due respect and compassion as other pets deserve the same. I read that George MacDonald, a Scottish minster who influenced the life and writings of C. Lewis, commented about "beasts" (animals) and God seeing the depth of their being in a way we cannot know. Our God is so big with the capacity to embrace all life- sparrows, sheep, lions, horses, etc. - as referenced in the Psalms and other Old Testament Scripture as well in the New Testament. The relationship we have with each other is greatly enhanced by God and all creation. As a poet said "All creatures great and small….The Lord God made them all."

The door has closed to another part of family life. Sometimes, for no apparent reason, the door opens in my mind as if it is a closet completely packed with remembrances of long-forgotten moments. A flood of events fills my thinking and, once again, special days are resurrected. As the thoughts overflow I am glad. Life is good.

I miss our feline family as I miss all the family. But I know caring for another kitty, because I am older and alone, is not really feasible, at least the way one should be taken care of. However, on the shelf is placed a bag of dry cat food. Who knows when another irresistible furry face with whiskers and pointed ears will appear on the outside of the family room French doors and ....

Made in the USA
Middletown, DE
19 April 2022